Tips for Better Government Documents (Microsoft Word 365)

Billy Morris

Introduction

Government writing is not academic or business writing. The government has a way of over emphasizing some rules and ignoring others. If you want to get it right, then find out what the policy is where you work. In my opinion a government document should be consistent and have structure. The purpose of this book is to teach basic structure.

As I write these instructions, I am using Office 365 so some of the Icons and the some of the instructions may not be the same in other version of Microsoft Word. I am going to use Icons and text to explain what you need to do to have professional looking documents. The instructions here should work with Office 2007 and above.

A well written document in any environment should consist of the following three parts

- Something to say to a specific audience

- Grammatically correct in accordance to the rules of that environment
- Structured so that it looks professional and is easy to read

The purpose of this book is to teach you how to set up structure so that you have a professional looking document that is easy to read.

It has taken me thirty years to learn what I know about Microsoft Word and even then, I am fairly sure there is a lot that I don't know. Anyone can use Microsoft Word and I guess that is why so many people use it. I have heard that all it really takes is playing around with the program so that you know where everything is. If this was true, then people would not have so much trouble even after using Microsoft Word for years.

Tips for Better Government Documents (Microsoft Word) is a short book to teach the basics of formatting a professional looking document that is easy to read. This book will discuss some general formatting rules, some government standards, some general tips, numbering, tables, table of contents, headers & footers and some extra content to include the navigation pane and the quick parts. The book uses a consistent method of instructions and images to teach the above basics of Microsoft Word.

First, I would like to explain who I am. I joined the Air Force in 1989. Even in the early nineties when there were only three computers for several dozen people, no one knew how to structure a basic document, but everyone had an opinion on how it should look. The later part of my career I worked as contracting specialist or officer (a very document heavy career field). I have worked in several headquarters from Numbered Air Forces to Combatant Commands. After retiring from the Air Force, I worked for several Army Units and even the Department of State.

Numbering

Table of Content

General Rules 1
    General Rules 2
    Tips 3
    Document Rules 4
General Formatting 6
    Army Standard 7
    Air Force Standards 8
    DOD Standards 9
    Date and Time Standards 10
    Font 11
    Spacing 13
    Set the Default 17
    Blank Document or Addition Text 17
General Tips 20
    Keyboard Shortcuts 20
    Basic Document 22
    Clipboard 24

Numbering

Numbering 28
   Turning Off Automatic Numbering 28
   Setup 29
   Instructional Text 30
   Instructions 32
   Adding Sections 39
   Basic Method 39
   Simplest Method 39
   Best Method 40
Tables 42
   Rules 42
   Sample 43
   Other Uses for Tables 50
   Pictures with or without Text 50
   Replacement for Columns 55
   Forms 55
Table of Contents 58
   Manual Tables 58
   Rules 59
   Instructions 60
   Adding Style Formatting 63

Numbering

- Second Table of Contents 66
- Primary Method...................................70
- Quick Method......................................70
- Updating the Table of Contents 71
- Headers and Footer 73
  - Editing Headers or Footers..................73
  - Text..75
  - Page Numbering...................................75
  - Pictures..78
  - Tables 78
  - Sections Breaks 80
- Extra 83
  - Navigation Pane 83
  - Water Marks 85
  - Signatures..86
  - Line Numbers 88
  - Quick Parts 88

Section 1 – General Rules

General Rules

Government writing is not academic or business writing. The government has a way of over emphasizing some rules and ignoring others. If you want to get it right, then find out what the policy is where you work. In my opinion a government document should be consistent and have structure. The purpose of this book is to teach basic structure.

As I write these instructions, I am using Office 365 so some of the Icons and the some of the instructions may vary from the version of Microsoft Word that you are using. I am going to use Icons and text to explain what you need to do to have professional looking documents. The instructions here should work with Office 2007 and above.

Section 1 – General Rules

General Rules

I am going to try to include some regulations and guides as I find them. However, most of these regulations and guides are outdated and my purpose here is to teach you how to structure and/or format a document to match the guidance of your organization. In my experience what is most in developing a professional government document is that the document is consistent and structured. For example:

- If you use the acronym DoD or DOD then every time you refer to the Department of Defense then use the same acronym (do not mix DoD with DOD and if you use a Table of Acronyms make sure that it matches with what you chose to use)
- Pick a date format and stick with it. The DOD likes to use the format did mmm yyyy for example 1 Jan 2019. However lately I have seen January 1, 2019
- Leadership may not understand how to format a document, but they absolutely know how to point out

Section 1 – General Rules

>that on page 1 you said you needed 10 units but now on page 10 you say that you now need 100 units. I would suggest keeping the important information in Excel or OneNote instead of trying to piece it together from several documents.

- Always be as direct and as formal as you can.
- Use a professional font such as "Times New Roman or Arial"
- Add a space before and after each paragraph

Tips

There are also a few steps that you can take as you set the documents that will make it easier to format your document such as:

- Establish rules for the document before you start because it is easier to set up a document as you go rather than to reformate
- Even though you establish rules before you start the document, write or format

Section 1 – General Rules

Document Rules

For this book, I will use the following rules:

- Font – Times New Roman – 12-points
- Singled spaced with a blank line before and after each paragraph
- I am going to use the < symbol to identify Microsoft Group item (items that are on the ribbon at the top of the page)
- I am going to use the > symbol to identify keys on the keyboard
- When I use just a letter such as A, I don't mean capital A but just the key A
- I am going to use "Text" to identify titles, drop down items or selected items
- I am going to indent bullets 1/4"
- I am going to use square bullets for instructions
- I am going to use round bullets for rules that I think you should follow
- I am going to indent text 1/2"
- I am going to indent pictures 1/2"

Section 1 – General Rules

- I am going to indent tables 1/4"
- I am going to end every section with a section break
- I am only using three levels when numbering or setting up a table of contents
- For headings, pictures titles and table titles, I am going to bold the Font

I am going to use the above rule so that I can teach you how to do professional documents.

Section 2 – General Formatting

General Formatting

The easiest way to get your document to look professional is to add structure to the document. With that said most government organizations have some kind of regulation on formatting document.

There is expression that say this is not grandfather's typewriter which is probably true for grammar, but this is your grandfather's government. Most grammar rules apply to government writing and if you are interested in better writing there are thousands of grammar books. However, something the government overstress such as capitalization. For example, you should only capitalize proper names but most government agency will capitalize any noun that refers to a person or place such as commander, contractor or main grate.

Section 2 – General Formatting

Army Standard

The Army Regulation for memorandums and office correspondence is "Army Regulation 25–50 Preparing and Managing Correspondence" dated 17 May 2013.

This regulation prescribes Department of the Army (DA) policies, procedures, and standard formats for preparing and processing Army correspondence.

When creating official correspondence, use the basic rules below to make the correspondence easy to read and understand. The following guidelines will provide the best results:

- A font with a point-size of 12 is recommended.
- Preferred type font is Arial.
- Unusual type styles, such as Script, will not be used in official correspondence
- Sometimes you will see a variety of color in Letterhead (see Army Regulation 25–30 for Letterhead), but the text in the body of final

Section 2 – General Formatting

document will almost always be black.

Air Force Standards

The Air Force Regulation for communication (spoken and written) is "Air Force Handbook 33-337 Communications and Information" or "The Tongue and Quill" dated 27 May 2015.

This handbook, together with Air Force Manual (AFMAN) 33-326, Preparing Official Communications, provides the information to ensure clear communications—written or spoken.

- A font with a point-size of 12 is recommended
- Preferred type font is Times New Roman or Courier New
- Unusual type styles, such as Script, will not be used in official correspondence
- Do not use bold, italic, script, or other unusual typefaces

Section 2 – General Formatting

DOD Standards

The DOD Regulation for Written Material is "Department of Defense Manual 5110.04 Volume 1 and 2" dated 19 April 2017.

This Manual reissues DoD 5110.4-M (Reference (a)) in accordance with the authority in DoD Directives 5105.53 and 5110.4 5105.82 and the Deputy Secretary of Defense Memorandum to provide guidance for managing the correspondence of the Secretary of Defense Deputy Secretary of Defense and Executive Secretary of the Department of Defense as well as OSD and DoD Component correspondence.

- Use Times New Roman, 12-point
- Single space within a paragraph
- Use a 2-inch top margin and 1-inch side and bottom margins on the first page
- Do not number the first page
- Correspondence may be signed in blue or black ink
- Black ink will be used for date stamps

Section 2 – General Formatting

Date and Time Standards

- Express dates on memorandums in the following formats: 1 January 2013 or 1 Jan 13.
- The four digits for the year will be used only when the month is spelled out or when date stamps use abbreviated months and four-digit year.
- Avoid separating any of the three date elements (day, month, and year) from each other. If absolutely necessary, the four-digit year may be carried over to the next line.
- Do not use postscripts in Army correspondence
- Military time will be expressed in a group of four digits, from 0001 to 2400, based on the 24–hour clock system

All government agencies probably have a policy or a regulation about document formatting. However, most of the time they are hard to find, vague or easy to be misinterpret. If the policy is readily

Section 2 – General Formatting

available, then you should use it even if it seems to contradict general grammar rules.

The higher a document goes in the chain of command the more people will care about what font you use or is your spacing write. However, you should try to have professional looking document no matter what level they are being review because you don't know where it will go, and people will judge you if it looks like a third grader did it.

Font

The font is the easiest place to start when you are creating a professional looking document. In my opinion there are only four (4) fonts that should be used in government documents

1. Times New Roman
2. Courier New
3. Calibri
4. Arial

I prefer Times New Roman probable because I severed in the Air Force. The Army prefers Arial. Courier New is used a

Section 2 – General Formatting

lot in older documents and Calibri is a modern font used a lot in business.

- The font size should be 12-point or smaller except for cover or title page but not less than 10-point
- The entire document should have the same font size except for cover or title page
- The font color for the body of the document should be black
- The body of the document should be single spaced with a line with a blank line between paragraphs

If you need to reduce the font to make additional space, you don't have to reduce it by a whole point for example:

- On the < Home Tab on the < Font Group you can see the current setting for 12-point size looks like this

- Type 11.5 instead of using the dropdown and your font size will be 11.5-point

Section 2 – General Formatting

If you just want to use a standard size do the following

- On the < Font Group select the size you want from the dropdown list

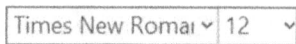

To change all the text at once do the following:

- Hold the > Ctrl Key
- Hit the > A Key
- Let go of the > Ctrl Key and the > A Key
- Follow the steps above

Spacing

To set the spacing do the following:

- On the < Home Tab on the < Paragraph Group
- Click the following Icon

The following menu will come up

Section 2 – General Formatting

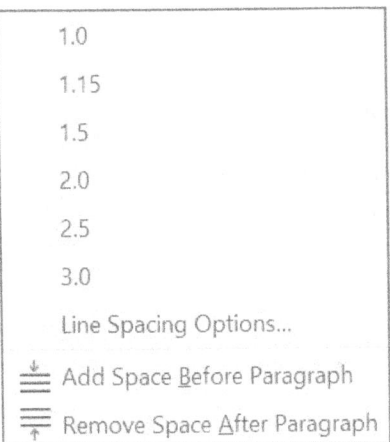

- Click "1.0"
- Repeat the steps above except this time
- Click "Add Space After Paragraph"

This is the foundation for a standard paragraph – single space with a line after the paragraph. You do not need a space before and after because that will give you too large of a gap between paragraphs. You could select "Add Space Before Paragraph" and this would give the correct spacing between paragraphs except your top line would be too low. If you need to fill space, you could select "1.15" instead of "1.0". This uses more space, but most people cannot tell the

Section 2 – General Formatting

difference. To be honest "1.15" looks better. The same trick works if you need additional space change "1.15" to "1.0".

The space after the paragraph can also be adjusted by doing the following

- On the < Home Tab on the < Paragraph Group
- Click the following Icon

The following menu will come up

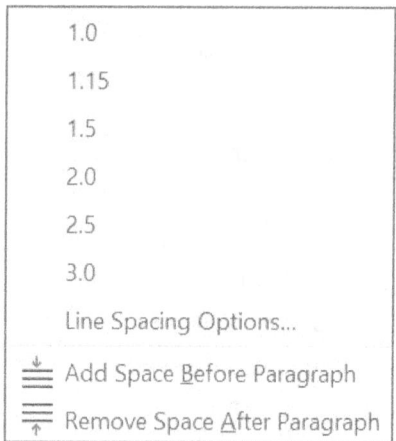

- Click "Line Spacing Options…"

The following menu will come up

15

Section 2 – General Formatting

The default spacing is 8-point. Again, this can be adjusted to meet the spacing requirements, but large changes will be noticeable. From this menu you can adjust your alignment or line spacing.

Section 2 – General Formatting

**Note: Changes to the line spacing or the spacing after the paragraph should be applied to the whole document not just the section where you need the space.

Set the Default

Now that you have the font and spacing correct it is time to set the default for normal style

- Highlight a section of text that includes a space after the paragraph
- On the < Home Tab on the < Styles Group
- Right click "Normal"
- Select "Normal to Match Selection" (now every time you add normal text you will not have to format it)

Blank Document or Addition Text

If you are starting with a blank document, then you can format the first word or even letter that you type and the rest of the document will be the same unless you change it so you don't have to set the default. This includes but is not limited to font, spacing or tab settings.

Section 2 – General Formatting

For example, if you if you set the font at Times New Roman with a font size of 12-point, line spacing at 1.15 with blank a space after the paragraph and a half inch tab stop. Then for the rest of your document if you do not change it then you have a basic letter format where every time you hit the Enter Key you will start a new paragraph that has 1.15 spacing, a blank line after the paragraph and the is indented by half an inch.

The above paragraph is also true if you are adding additional text to you document. Everything that you type after the addition of text will match your selected format until you change it or start typing somewhere else in document and then Word will match the format of the section you click to.

**Note: Once you have the format the way you want it you can set the format to default by doing the following:

- On the < Home Tab on the < Font Group right
- Then click the following Icon (in the right-hand corner)

Section 2 – General Formatting

- When the menu comes up select set as default

Section 3 – General Tips

General Tips

Anything that saves you time or effort is worth learning. In the following section I am going to discuss keyboard shortcut, basic structure, using the clipboard and how to keep track of the facts that you use in your documents.

Keyboard Shortcuts

Select Whole Document

- Hold the > Ctrl Key
- Hit the > A Key
- Release both Keys

Copy Text

- Highlight text
- Hold the > Ctrl Key
- Hit the > C Key
- Release both Keys

Paste Text

Section 3 – General Tips

- Place the cursor where you want the text
- Hold the > Ctrl Key
- Hit the > V Key
- Release both Keys

Cut Text

- Highlight text
- Hold the > Ctrl Key
- Hit the > X Key
- Release both Keys

Undo

- Hold the > Ctrl Key
- Hit the > Z Key
- Release both Keys

Repeat

- Hold the > Ctrl Key
- Hit the > Y Key
- Release both Keys

Bold

- Highlight text
- Hold the > Ctrl Key
- Hit the > B Key
- Release both Keys

Section 3 – General Tips

Italic

- Highlight text
- Hold the > Ctrl Key
- Hit the > I Key
- Release both Keys

Underline

- Highlight text
- Hold the > Ctrl Key
- Hit the > U Key
- Release both Keys

** Note: There are dozens of shortcuts, but the ones listed above are the most common but if you are interested in learning additional shortcuts you can do an internet search to find additional shortcut list. One of the best that I have found is at https://darnoffice.com/microsoft-office-shortcuts/

Basic Document

There are two major parts to a professional document.

The first part to a professional document is readability which includes grammar, flow

Section 3 – General Tips

and direction your document to match your audience. Other things that you should consider are what are you trying to say and is the information consistent.

There are thousands of books on grammar. However, you may have to research to find one that you like and trust. There are more than a few methods on flow and probably a ton of books on this. I think the Air Force's "Tongue and Quill does a fairly good job when it comes to government writing.

Before you write the first word, you should know what you want to say and who your audience is.

The second part to a professional document is formatting and structure which includes spacing, font, numbering and general appearance. Again, your formatting and structure should be consistent and be planned out.

Most of this book is about structure and formatting which leaves consistency. Depending on the size of your document, the information in it could come from a dozen

Section 3 – General Tips

different sources which is why it is so hard to be consistent.

An easy solution for this is to create a fact sheet for every project that you have. By fact sheet, I mean a simple document that you can use as a reference. I have used Word, Excel and even Notepad but I think the best program is Microsoft's OneNote which contains tabs like Excel and you can place your data any similar to PowerPoint but still give you the text editing that you have in Word.

Once you have collected the information you still need to transfer it to your document. You could use the shortcuts above to copy/paste the information as need or you could copy everything into Microsoft's clipboard.

Clipboard

The clipboard is the most under used function in the entire Microsoft family of products. To open the clipboard, do the following:

Section 3 – General Tips

- On the < Home Tab in < Clipboard Group
- Click the following Icon

**Note: You will have to click in the right-hand corner

You can copy and store up to twenty-four (24) unique items to include images, text and cells into the clipboard so that you can paste them back into your document at any time in any order.

Below is an image of some instructional text

Section 3 – General Tips

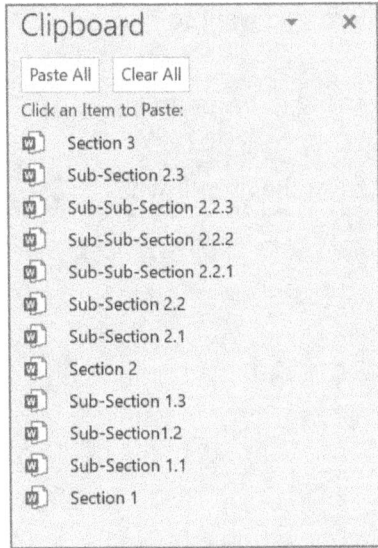

To use the clipboard, do the following:

- Place the cursor where you want to add an image, text or the content a cell from the clipboard
- Click the image, text or the content a cell that you want from the clipboard

**Note: The items on the clipboard can be pasted anywhere in the document in any order.

You can remove any item from the clipboard by doing the following

Section 3 – General Tips

- Scroll over the item you want to remove
- Click the down arrow to bring up a dropdown
- Select "Delete" from the dropdown

Section 4 – Numbering

Numbering

There are many advantages to using the built-in numbering system such as

- If you add or remove a section of text, then Microsoft will update your numbering
- Looks better and is far more consistent looking
- Using the built-in numbering system could save hours and hours of your time.

However, working with numbering and bullets can be very tricky because no matter when or where you try to number or insert bullets Microsoft tries to guess what you want. If your document is small or simple, then this might even be helpful.

Turning Off Automatic Numbering

If you have a simple structure and you are having trouble with Microsoft changing the

Section 4 – Numbering

numbering, you can turn off the Automatic Numbering by doing the following:

- Select < File
- Select < Options
- Select < Proofing
- Select < AutoCorrect Options…
- Select the Tab < AutoFormat As You Type tab
- Uncheck the box < Automatic numbered lists check box
- Then click < OK

**Note: In most cases I believe it is a waste of time to turn off the automatic numbering and you are better off learning how to do it correctly.

Setup

Normally, before I start setting up the numbering, I will select all the text in entire document and remove all formatting.

I will then setup the headings. For example, for the main sections 1.0, 2.0, 3.0 etc.… I will set as Heading 1 and for the sub sections, I will set as Heading 2 or Heading 3. I think it looks very unprofessional to go

Section 4 – Numbering

more than 3 levels, so I don't number after the third level. However, I will teach you to go as many levels as you. You don't have to clear the formatting or setup levels but to clear all formatting do the following:

- Hold the > Ctrl Key
- Hit the > A Key
- Release both Keys

This will select everything in your document. To clear the formatting do the following:

- On the < Home Tab in < Font Group
- Click the following Icon

   Clear All Formatting

Again, you do not have to set up Heading or clear the formatting, but I like to start with a clean document.

Generally, this is a good time to setup a basic line spacing structure. To setup the line spacing follow the instructions for spacing in the General Formatting Section.

Instructional Text

Section 4 – Numbering

I am going to start with a small group of meaningless words to show you how to go from a block of text to numbered sections of text. I am going then separate the words and remove the period because phases used as headers do not have punctuation. To setup the line spacing follow the instructions for spacing in the General Formatting Section.

Section 1. Sub-Section 1.1. Sub-Section1.2. Sub-Section 1.3. Section 2. Sub-Section 2.1. Sub-Section 2.2. Sub-Sub-Section 2.2.1. Sub-Sub-Section 2.2.2. Sub-Sub-Section 2.2.3. Sub-Section 2.3. Section 3.

Separate the above text by placing the cursor before each section title and hitting > Enter. When you are complete, it should look similar to what I have below.

Section 1

Sub-Section 1.1

Sub-Section1.2

Sub-Section 1.3

Section 2

Section 4 – Numbering

Sub-Section 2.1

Sub-Section 2.2

Sub-Sub-Section 2.2.1

Sub-Sub-Section 2.2.2

Sub-Sub-Section 2.2.3

Sub-Section 2.3

Section 3

Instructions

- Highlight Section 1
- On the < Home Tab in < Paragraph Group
- Click the following Icon

       Numbering

- Select any numbering style. I selected the following:

- Highlight Section 2

Section 4 – Numbering

- On the < Home Tab in < Paragraph Group
- Click the following Icon

  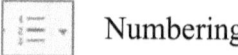 Numbering

- Select the same numbering style as before.
- Repeat the steps above for Section 3

** Note: you can select all section at once by holding down the > Ctrl Key and mouse clicking on the text that you want to add. Once you have everything that you want to number highlighted then follow the steps above.

- Click on the first number (it will highlight)
- On the < Home Tab in < Paragraph Group
- Click the following Icon

  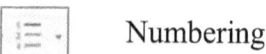 Numbering

- At the bottom of the menu
- Select "Define New Number Format…"
- The following menu will come up

Section 4 – Numbering

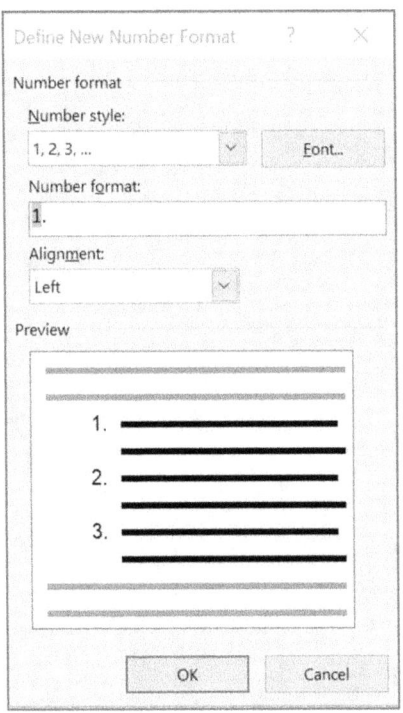

- In the field Number format: change 1. To 1.0 (make sure to leave the 1 by moving the curser to the right and adding the zero.

**Note: As I have done this, I have also adjusted the list indention by right clicking on the number and selecting "Adjust List Indent…"

Section 4 – Numbering

- By this point, what you have should like the section below

1.0 Section 1

Sub-Section 1.1

Sub-Section1.2

Sub-Section 1.3

2.0 Section 2

Sub-Section 2.1

Sub-Section 2.2

Sub-Sub-Section 2.2.1

Sub-Sub-Section 2.2.2

Sub-Sub-Section 2.2.3

Sub-Section 2.3

3.0 Section 3

- Highlight Sub-Section 1.1, Sub-Section 1.2 and Sub-Section 1.3

** Note: You can do this by holding the > Ctrl Key and clicking on all the Sub-Sections in Section 1.0.

Section 4 – Numbering

- On the < Home Tab in < Paragraph Group
- Click the following Icon

   Numbering

- Select any numbering style other than the one that you selected for Sections 1, 2 and 3. I selected the following

- Click on the first number (it will highlight)
- Click the following Icon on the <Home Tab in <Paragraph Group

  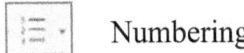 Numbering

- At the bottom of the menu
- Select "Define New Number Format…"
- The following menu will come up

Section 4 – Numbering

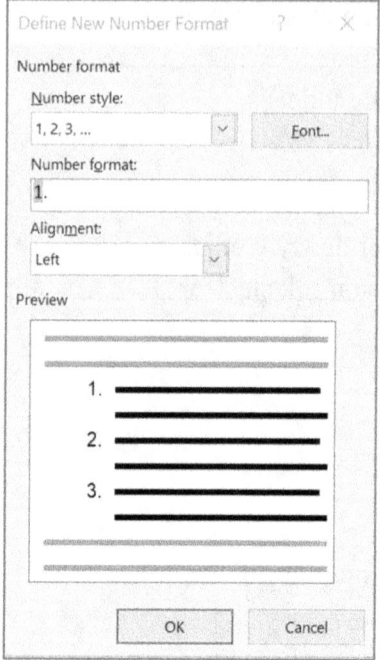

- Change the Number Style to match the one you used for Section 1, 2, and 3
- In the field "Number format:" change 1. To 1.1 (make sure to leave the 1 by moving the curser to the left and adding 1 and period.
- Repeat for each of the sections and sub-sections.

Section 4 – Numbering

- I have also adjusted the list indention by right clicking on the number and selecting "Adjust List Indent..."
- By this point, what you have should like the section below

1.0 Section 1

1.1 Sub-Section 1.1

1.2 Sub-Section1.2

1.3 Sub-Section 1.3

2.0 Section 2

2.1 Sub-Section 2.1

2.2 Sub-Section 2.2

2.2.1 Sub-Sub-Section 2.2.1

2.2.2 Sub-Sub-Section 2.2.2

2.2.3 Sub-Sub-Section 2.2.3

Section 4 – Numbering

2.3   Sub-Section 2.3

3.0   Section 3

**Note: If you delete a section the numbers will adjust.

Adding Sections

Most people have trouble adding sections and getting the numbering to pick up correctly. There are several ways to do this.

Basic Method

You could place the additional text between the numbered sections and follow the steps above to number the additional text.

**Note: If the numbering is only one level or very simple this will work. However, most of the time Microsoft makes a bad guess and you end up with a miss-numbered section that is hard to fix. If you need to add an additional level of numbering, make sure that you choose a different style and then go back and change it.

Simplest Method

Section 4 – Numbering

The simplest method to add a section is to go to the last section that is numbered correctly. Go to the end of the sentence after the punctuation and hit > Enter.

This will pick up the numbering from the previous paragraph. However, this only works if the previous sentence or paragraph is numbered and you do not need text between numbered sections. You could always copy/cut the text that you need between your numbered sections and paste it back after you are finished with the numbering.

Best Method

The best method is to place the text where you need it and use the Format Painter to match the numbering that you need.

This is how you use the Format Painter

- Add the text you need
- Highlight the numbered section that you want to match
- On the < Home Tab in < Clipboard Group

Section 4 – Numbering

- Click the following Format Painter Icon

  Format Painter

- Now highlight the section that you want to number

Section 5 – Tables

Tables

Tables are very simple objects that provide a method of organizing your data into professional presentations.

Rules

Rules for making tables look professional

- The table margins should not exceed the text margins
- Be consistent
- The text in the table should centered in most cases
- If your tables have headers, then they should all match
- If you use a fill color, then you should use the same colors scheme in all your tables
- Use the same font as the body of text that is not in the table
- Text in a cell should not touch the sides or top and bottom

Section 5 – Tables

Sample

I am going to start with a simple 4X4 table.

To insert a table, do the following:

- On the < Insert Tab in < Tables Group
- Click the following Icon

- Scroll down and to the right until you have 4X4 table
- Click to select

Section 5 – Tables

I like to have the Ruler turned on at the top of the page.

To turn Ruler on do the following:

- On the < View Tab in < Show Group
- Check the following Box

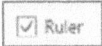

- Click in the table, you will get the following symbol in the upper left corner of the table

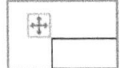

- Click the cross symbol to highlight the entire table

You can now use the ruler at the top of the page to adjust location of the table and the size of the columns. I select the following

The above method is an easy way to make simple adjustment to the table. You can also right click on the table and select < Table Properties… or pick other basic function on

Section 5 – Tables

the menu. For more complex formatting use the < Design or < Layout Tabs

If you click just to the left of a row or just above the column you can highlight the entire Row or Column

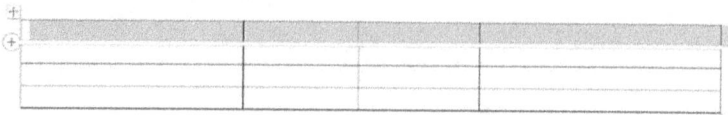

**Note: You can also add rows or columns by clicking the following Icon on the left side or top of the Table

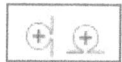

**Note: To delete a row or column, highlight the row or column and right click the highlighted area and select delete.

Using the < Design and < Layout Tabs, I have formatted the basic table above to the table below

Section 5 – Tables

Name	Quantity	Unit of Issue	Cost per Unit	Total
Text	1	Each	$10.00	$10.00
Text	2	Each	$5.00	$10.00
Text	3	Each	$1.00	$3.00

Table 1

To make the table above, I did the following:

- Click the following Icon on the top side of the table to add a column

- Add text to each cell
- Filling the top row by highlighting the row
- On the < Design Tab in the < Table Styles Group
- Select the following Icon

- Select a color from the menu

Section 5 – Tables

**Note: You could also fill the row by doing the following

- On the < Home Tab in the < Paragraph Group
- Select the following Icon

- Select a color from the menu
- Centered the text by
- Highlighting the entire table by clicking the following Icon on the upper left corner of the table

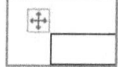

- Then on the < Layout Tab in the < Alignment Group
- Selected the following Icon

- Then on the < Layout Tab in the < Alignment Group
- Selected the following Icon

Section 5 – Tables

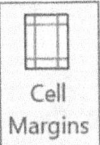

- For the table above, I set the margins as follows

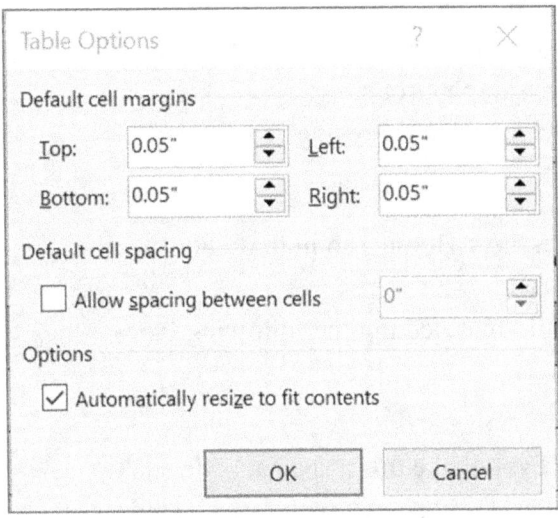

- Highlighted the top row by clicking to the left of the top row
- On the < Home Tab in the < Font Group
- Bold the entire top row by selecting the following Icon

Section 5 – Tables

- Add a table title at the bottom of the table.

Center and bold the text by

- Highlighting the text
- Then on the < Home Tab in the < Paragraph Group
- Selected the following Icon

- On the < Home Tab in the < Font Group
- Bold by selecting the following Icon

**Note: If you make this a special style such as Title later, I will show you how to include this in a table of content.

It does not take a lot of time to make a table look better and to make it easier to read. However, as with most professional writing if you go to fancy then it will start to look like a third grader did.

Section 5 – Tables

Other Uses for Tables

Table are very useful for adding for adding structure to a document. For example

- Tables can be used to center and align picture with or without text
- Tables can be used instead of using the columns
- Tables can be used to structure your document into a form or add blank lines that do not shift

Pictures with or without Text

Inserted a 2X2 table using the method above

- Insert an image in 3 of the 4 cells

There are several ways to insert an image such as:

- Make sure the cursor is in the cell you want the image
- On the < Insert Tab in the < Illustration Group
- Selected the following Icon

Section 5 – Tables

- Find an image and click "Insert"

Or

- Paste an image into the cell

Or

- Drag an image into the cell from somewhere else in the document

When you complete with the images

- Add text to the remaining cell

By this point what you have should be similar to what I have below

|  | The images in this table are from another book that I wrote a couple of years ago. The book is called This is part of the cover of a book that I wrote a few year ago |

Section 5 – Tables

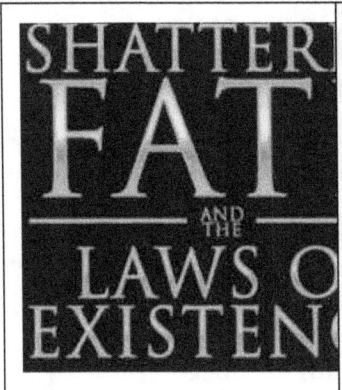 

The pictures are aligned without having to deal with whether or not the image is in line with the text or not.

The pictures can also be resized within the boundaries of the table by doing the following:

- Click on the image and you will get a box with small circle on that is similar to the image below

Section 5 – Tables

- Then click and hold one of the small circles along the edge of the image
- Drag the small circle until the image is the desired size

Once you are finished formatting the images, remove the borders by doing the following:

- Click in the table, you will get the following symbol in the upper left corner of the table

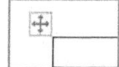

- Click the cross symbol to highlight the entire table
- On the < Home Tab in the < Paragraph Group
- Selected the following Icon

Section 5 – Tables

- From the drop down select "No Border"

By this point you should have something similar to what I have below

The images in this table are from another book that I wrote a couple of years ago. The book is called "Shattered Fate and the Laws of Existence."

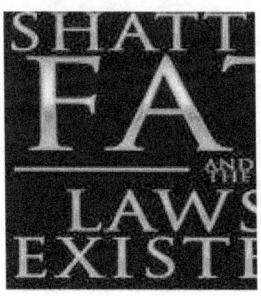

Section 5 – Tables

You can drag the images in or out of the table and if you move the table you move all the images at once.

Replacement for Columns

The above technic can be used to replace columns

- Insert a 3X1 table
- Add some text
- Add some bullets if you like
- Remove borders using the steps above

▪ Bullet 1	• List 1	○ Statement 1
▪ Bullet 2	• List 2	○ Statement 2
▪ Bullet 3	• List 3	○ Statement 3

Forms

You can use tables to create forms by using the Merge Cells and Split Cells function on the < Layout Tab in the < Merge Group

Section 5 – Tables

For example

Last Name		First Name	
Age		Reference #	12345678
Date			

You can add a border to all sides or any one of the sides. This is useful if you need a blank line for someone to input information

- Insert a 3X5 table
- Add some text
- Add some bullets if you like
- Remove borders using the steps above

Name		Date
Rank		Office

Section 5 – Tables

- Remove borders

Name						Date

Rank						Office

- Select the cell above the text
- Add a bottom border to the cells above the text
- Center text

Name	Date

Rank	Office

**Note: Not only does this look very nice, but the lines will not shift, move or split when you type on them

Section 6 – Table of Contents

Table of Contents

A table of contents can help to make your document look professional and make it easier for someone else to find information in your document. However, if it is not done right, they are a real time killer that can make your document look like a third grader wrote it.

Manual Tables

A manual table is any table of content where you build a table or a list of the section without any assistance from Microsoft. Downfalls of using a manual table of contents verse an automated table using Microsoft Quick Parts

- Depending on the size of your document it could take an hour to setup a table of contents
- You have to figure out how to format a table so that it looks professional

Section 6 – Table of Contents

- Depending on where in your document or how much you change now you have to figure how to keep track of the changes so you can update the table of contents

Rules

Rules for setting up before you even start the table of contents

- Decide how many levels want
- Decide what kind of heading you want
- Decide if you need more than one table of contents (additional tables of contents could be for images or tables)

Setting up the document for a table of content as you set the document is by far the best way to go. First, I am going to show you how to set up for a table of content as you go. Then, I will show you how to set up for a table of content on a document that is already setup.

- I don't believe documents should have than 3 levels of numbering so

Section 6 – Table of Contents

> for this lesson I am only going to use 3 levels.
> - I am going to use heading 1, heading 2 and heading 3 for this lesson.
> - I am also going to use Title Styles for tables and images which means I am going to have 2 tables of contents

Instructions

In the section below select the highest level for the table of content. In this case I am going to select Section 1, Section 2 and Section 3

Either one at a time or all at once by holding the > Ctrl Button and clicking on each section of text that you want to be Heading 1

Section 1

Sub-Section 1.1

Sub-Section1.2

Sub-Section 1.3

Section 2

Sub-Section 2.1

Sub-Section 2.2

Section 6 – Table of Contents

Sub-Sub-Section 2.2.1

Sub-Sub-Section 2.2.2

Sub-Sub-Section 2.2.3

Sub-Section 2.3

Section 3

- On the < Home Tab in the < Styles Group
- Select "Heading 1"

**Note: You may have to format the text after you select "Heading 1". I selected Times New Roman Font size 12 and front color black and bold

Once you have the formatting that you want, do the following to set a default for the style:

- Highlight the text
- On the < Home Tab in the < Styles Group
- Right click on the style that you want to update
- Select "Update Heading 1 to Match Selection" (now every time you add

Section 6 – Table of Contents

> another Heading 1 you will not have to format it)
- Repeat the steps above until you have something similar to what I have below

Section 1

Sub-Section 1.1

Sub-Section1.2

Sub-Section 1.3

Section 2

Sub-Section 2.1

Sub-Section 2.2

Sub-Sub-Section 2.2.1

Sub-Sub-Section 2.2.2

Sub-Sub-Section 2.2.3

Sub-Section 2.3

Section 3

- On the < Insert Tab in the < Text Group
- Select the following Icon

Section 6 – Table of Contents

 Quick Parts

When the dropdown menu comes up select the following Icon:

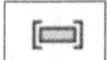 Field....

When the Field menu comes up select TOC. When the menu disappears the following table of content will appear:

```
Section 1 .................................... 16
    Sub-Section 1.1 ..................... 16
    Sub-Section 1.2 ..................... 16
    Sub-Section 1.3 ..................... 16
Section 2 .................................... 16
    Sub-Section 2.1 ..................... 16
    Sub-Section 2.2 ..................... 16
        Sub-Sub-Section 2.2.1 ........ 16
        Sub-Sub-Section 2.2.2 ........ 16
        Sub-Sub-Section 2.2.3 ........ 16
    Sub-Section 2.3 ..................... 16
Section 3 .................................... 16
```

Adding Style Formatting

If you are not starting with an unformatted document when add the formatting styles you can run into issue. In most situations if you are using a table of contents in your

Section 6 – Table of Contents

document then you are probably using numbering. The problem with this is the styles (Heading 1, Heading 2 etc....) that you use for the table of content has a default setting that does not include a number so when you add the style formatting you remove the numbering.

There are a few ways to approach this problem.

- First, add the style formatting using the steps above
- Add the numbering format back using one of the methods in the numbering section

The above method works but if you missed a section that you want to add to the table of contents or if you are adding additional text. However, if you are adding style formatting to a document that already has numbering formatting then you will need to do the steps above for every section, sub-section and sub-sub-sections. This sounds like a lot of work but in the long run it is quicker and looks better than a manual table of contents that you will never get perfect.

Section 6 – Table of Contents

A better method that I use for adding style formatting to a document that has already been numbered is by doing the following:

First, save a second copy of the document

- Open both documents

Clear all formatting in the original document by

- Holding the > Ctrl Key
- Hitting the > A Key
- Let go of the > Ctrl Key and the > A Key

**Note: This will select everything in your document.

To clear the formatting do the following:

- On the < Home Tab in < Font Group
- Click the following Icon

Now add the style formatting using the steps above

Add the numbering format back using one of the methods in the numbering section

Section 6 – Table of Contents

The purpose of the second document is so you have a reference of what the unformatted document should look like (numbering, font or anything else that you might have changed)

Second Table of Contents

The only difference between a table of content to list the sections the document and a table of content to list the images or tables is the styles that you allow.

To limit the styles, do the following:

- Highlight the table of content

**Note: You don't have to highlight the table but if you don't then you will have scroll down to TOC after the next step.

- Right click the table of content
- Select "Edit Field…" and the following menu will come up:

Section 6 – Table of Contents

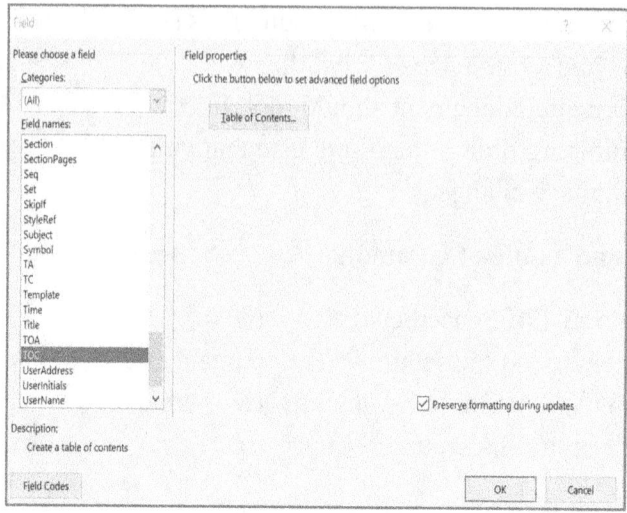

- Select the following button in the center of the menu

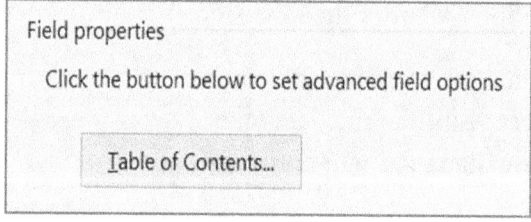

Once you click the above button the following menu will come up

Section 6 – Table of Contents

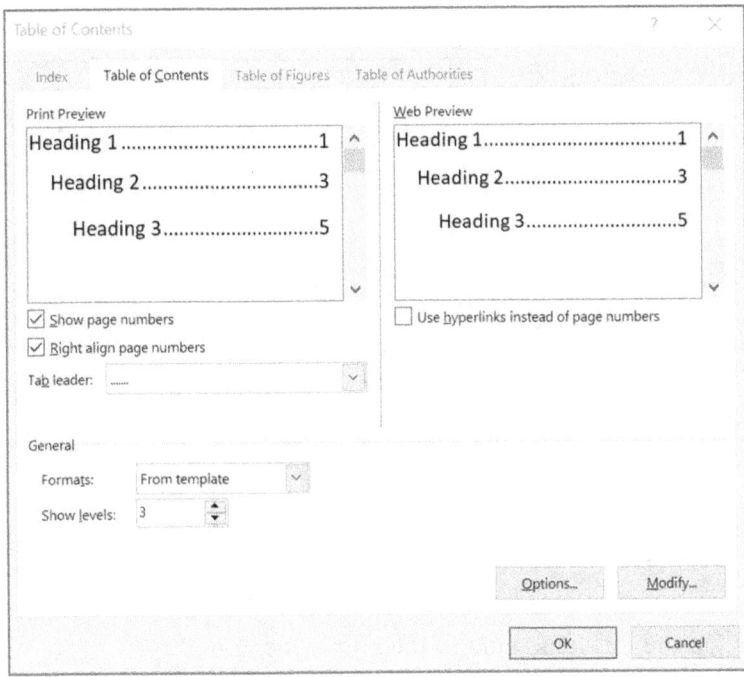

- In the lower left-hand corner of this menu "Show Level", you can set the number of levels (the default is 3)
- To set which 3 styles will show up in the table of contents select "Options…" in the lower right-hand corner

Section 6 – Table of Contents

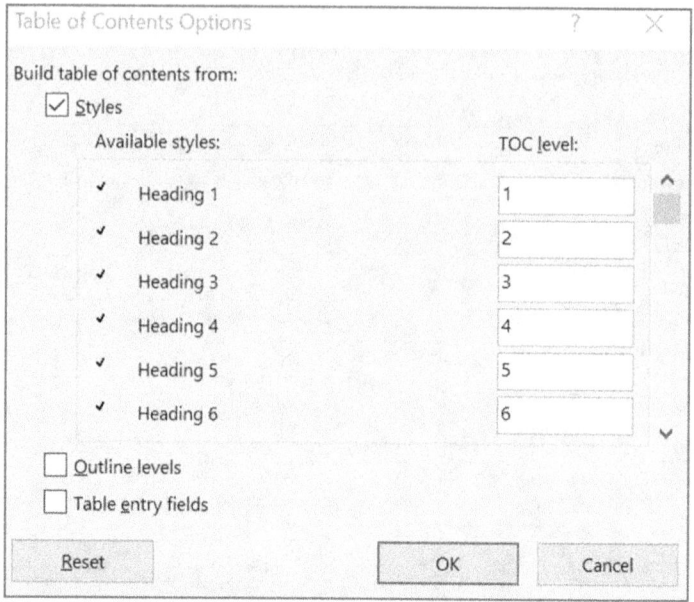

On the left-hand side of the above menu it lists the styles in your document. On the right-hand side of the menu is listed the order the style appears in the table of contents. If you remove the numbers, then the style will not show up in the table of content. Therefore, if you setup a second table and remove everything except the style you used for the table or image titles then you have a table of content not related to the first.

Section 6 – Table of Contents

To change the formatting of the table of content select "Modify…" The first menu only shows the formatting.

Primary Method

- Click "Modify…" to bring up the modification menu. From here you can change the table of content in any way that you would any other text.

Quick Method

You could also format the table of content by doing the following:

- Highlight the table of content
- On the < Home Tab in the < Font Group
- Select the changes you want to make

Or

- Right click on the text inside table of contents that you want to change, and formatting menu will come up

**Note: Although this method is much quicker, if you update the table of contents using the method below then you will have

Section 6 – Table of Contents

to reformat the table of contents every time you make an update.

Updating the Table of Contents

Once you are finished adding or removing content to your document it is time to update the table of content by doing the following:

- On the table of content
- Right click anywhere
- When the menu comes select "Update Field"

The following menu will come up

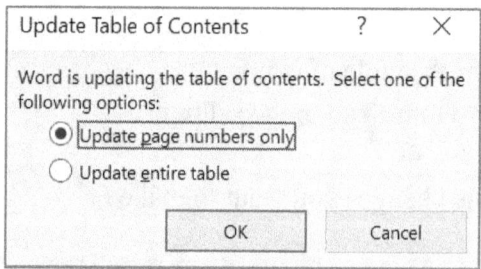

If you added or deleted text without adding formatting styles then select "Update page numbers only". However, if you have changes that add formatted style then you need to select "Update the entire table".

Section 6 – Table of Contents

**Note: I always select "Update the entire table" because I want to make sure that I don't miss anything, but if you format the table of content using the quick method you may have to update the formatting.

Section 8 – Section Breaks

Headers and Footer

Headers and footer allow you to provide additional information to your document such as title, page number or date. All formatting and most of the functions that you can do in the main body of the document can be done in ether of the headers or footers.

Editing Headers or Footers

There are several methods to changing the headers or footer.

Simple Method

- Double click anywhere in either the header or footer

Insert Method

- On the < Insert Tab in the < Header &Footer Group select Header or Footer

The following menu will come up

Section 8 – Section Breaks

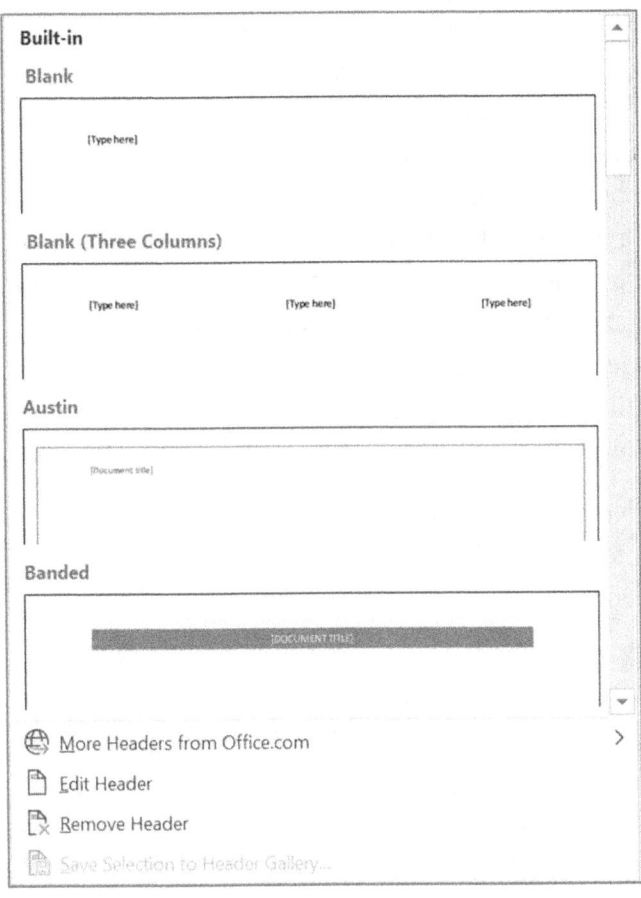

From this menu you could chose a built-in or on-line template for your header or footer but for this lesson I selected "Edit Header".

**Note: It works the same for footers

Section 8 – Section Breaks

Once you are in either the header or footer an additional tab called Headers & Footers will appear after the last tab on the ribbon. From this tab you can add some of the common item that you would normally find in a header or footer such as page number, date or field. You can also decide if you want different headers or footers on the first page. This is useful for large documents with title pages or if you need to create letterhead.

**Note: The formatting in the headers or footers works the same as the body of the document.

Text

To add text to either the header or footer

- Open the header or footer
- Start typing
- Justify left, right or center

**Note: You can have multiple lines of text in the header, footer or both.

Page Numbering

Section 8 – Section Breaks

There are at least two methods of add page numbers to the header or footer

- Open the header or footer
- On the < Headers & Footers Tab in the < Header &Footer Group
- Select "Page Number"
- For government documents select "Bottom of the Page"
- When the dropdown menu comes up select "Plain Number 3"

This will give a page number in your default text justified on the right side of the footer

- "Plain Number 1" will give a page number in your default text justified on the left side of the footer
- "Plain Number 2" will give a page number in your default text justified on the left side of the footer

The second method is

- Open the header or footer
- Select where you want the number
- On the < Insert Tab in the < Text Group select the following Icon

Section 8 – Section Breaks

 Quick Parts

- When the dropdown menu comes up select the following Icon:

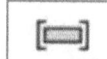 Field….

- When the Field menu comes up select "Page"
- Select the format for the number
- Click "OK"

Both methods will give a number that you can format, add text before or after and move within the footer.

Enhanced Method

- Open the footer
- Type Page x of x
- You can use either of the above methods above to add a page number instead of the second x
- You must use the second method to replace the first x except instead of choosing Page from the "Quick Parts" choose "NumPages"

Section 8 – Section Breaks

This will give the page number of the number of pages for example Page 5 of 10.

Pictures

There are several ways to insert an image such as:

- Make sure the cursor is in the footer or header where you want the image
- On the < Insert Tab in the < Illustration Group
- Selected the following Icon

- Find an image and click "Insert"

Or

- Paste an image into the footer or header where you want the image

Or

- Drag an image into the footer or header where you want the image from somewhere else in the document

Tables

Section 8 – Section Breaks

Anytime you want to structure your information, I think the easiest method is to use tables and the headers and footers are no exception.

To insert a table, do the following:

- Click the following Icon on the < Insert Tab in < Tables Group

- Scroll down and to the right until you have the size table you want
- Click to select

When you are done don't forget to hide the borders by doing the following

- Click in the table, you will get the following symbol in the upper left corner of the table

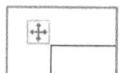

- Click the cross symbol to highlight the entire table

Section 8 – Section Breaks

- On the < Home Tab in the < Paragraph Group selected the following Icon

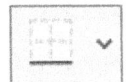

- From the drop down select "No Border"

Sections Breaks

Section breaks allow you to break your document into sections which does not sound like a big deal but when you are working with very large documents this is how add different headers and page numbers that are related to the section. For example, in this document I used section breaks to title each of my sections. You could PDF a bunch of smaller documents with different header and different page numbering but there is no reason why you could not do it in word.

To break your document into sections, do the following:

- Go to a blank line after where you want your section to end

Section 8 – Section Breaks

- Click the following Icon on the < Layout Tab in < Page Setup Section

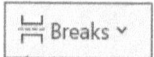

- When the drown down menu comes up select "Next Page"
- Double click in the header on the next page
- Click the following Icon on the < Header & Footer Tab in < Navigation Section

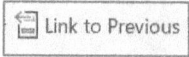

Once you click the Icon it will no longer be highlighted (this is how you know it is disabled)

- Double click in the footer on the next page
- Click the following Icon on the < Header & Footer Tab in < Navigation Section

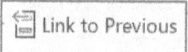

Section 8 – Section Breaks

Once you click the Icon it will no longer be highlighted (this is how you know it is disabled)

Now word will treat each section like a different document. You can change the header or footer in one or all of the sections without effecting the others.

Section 9 – Extra

Extra

The following items are additional functions to help make your document look better or functions that will make it easier to find your data in your document.

Navigation Pane

The navigation pane is one the most efficient tools in Microsoft Word and second only to the clipboard. The navigation pane does a much better job than the find or replace function and displays the same information that is in the table of contents.

There are several methods to display the navigation pane

Normal Method

- On the < View Tab in < Show Section
- Check the following Icon

    ☐ Navigation Pane

Section 9 – Extra

Quick Method

- Hold the > Ctrl Key
- Hit the > F Key
- Let go of the > Ctrl Key and the > F Key

Easy Method

- Click the lower left corner of the document where it says "Page x of x"

From the search bar in the navigation pane if you search for a key word or phrase then it will tell you the number of times the key word or phrase appears in the document. Word will highlight the heading in which the word or phrase appears. You can scroll through the navigation pane to exactly where you want to be in the document or click the Page Tab and word will show you the page that the word or phrase show up on. To get out of the search

- Click the X on the right-hand side of the search bar

Section 9 – Extra

The navigation pane will list the headings in your document. To go to anywhere in the document from the navigation pane

- Click the heading or sub-heading where you want to go

This will take you to that section of the document. You can also restructure the body of your document by

- Click the heading or sub-heading and holding the mouse button
- Drag the heading or sub-heading to where you want it

This will move all the text under the heading or sub-heading that you moved to the new location.

**Note: The navigation pane in Word does not display headings that are in tables, text boxes, or the headers or footers.

Water Marks

Water Marks are fairly straight forward except it is probably not where you think it would be. To add water marks, do the following:

Section 9 – Extra

- on the < Design Tab in < the Page Background Group
- Click the following Icon

The following menu will come up

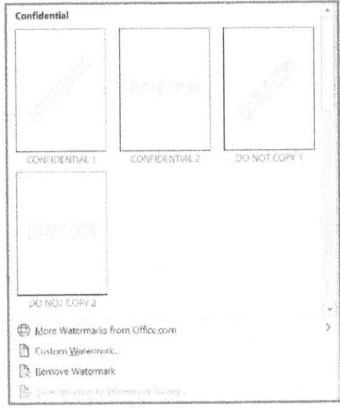

From this menu you can add any of the pre-installed water marks, upload a water mark or delete a water mark

Signatures

Microsoft Word offers a simple method to allow you to use your CAC to sign documents.

Section 9 – Extra

To insert a Signature Block, do the following

- Click the following Icon on the < Insert Tab in < the Text Group

**Note: There are limitations to this Signature Block such as if you change the document after you sign it then it will remove the signature, and this requires a CAC or Digital ID.

Other options include inserting an image of your signature. No matter what you do to the document the signature will stay but it is an image so it can be removed or copied very easily.

If you use this method, then when you are finished editing the document you should turn the document into a PDF by either saving as PDF or using the print to PDF.

**Note: The method above works very well instead of printing a document, sign it and scan it so that you can send it to someone.

Section 9 – Extra

Line Numbers

Line Numbering can help when several people are editing a large document. To add Line Numbers to the following

- On the < Layout Tab in the < Page Setup Groups
- Select the following Icon

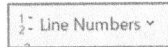

Quick Parts

Quick Parts consist of four elements that can be used to either to add function or are used to quickly add items to help your document look better.

AutoText

AutoText allow you to store information that you can reusable similar to the clipboard except it will still be there when you reopen the document. You can save information to AutoText by doing the following:

- Selecting the text, you want
- On the < Insert Tab in the < Text Group Groups
- Select the following Icon

Section 9 – Extra

 Quick Parts

When the dropdown menu comes up select the following Icon:

- Click "AutoText"
- Then clicking "Save Selection to AutoText Gallery"

**Note: This is very useful for storing long organizational name or common acronyms.

Document Property

Click Document Property to choose from a list of the document's properties.

**Note: You do not have to fill in the document property boxes with the information that is expected. You now have about 10 reference that you can use anywhere in your document.

For example: A large document may reuse things like project name or location over and over in the document but if this information changes then you have to find all the place where you have the old information and replace it with the new information.

Section 9 – Extra

However, if you enter the project name in the "Author" Reference you will be able to insert "Author" Reference instead of the project name. Now if you change the "Author" Reference to something else the Microsoft will update the entire document with the new information.

To update the Document Property, do the following

- Click the < File Tab
- In the Properties Section
- Update the Reference

Field

Microsoft field allow you to add code to your document that can be automatically updated.

There are about seventy-five field that can be used in Microsoft Word. The most common field are

- Date – allow you to insert a date that will update each time you open the document
- Page – shows the current page

Section 9 – Extra

- NumPage – shows the number of pages
- TOC – list the set of heading and the page number

For a complete list of Fields go to the following website

https://support.office.com/en-us/article/List-of-field-codes-in-Word-1ad6d91a-55a7-4a8d-b535-cf7888659a51

Useful shortcuts for Fields

Update or calculates selected Field

- Click > F9
- Release

Displays or hides selected Field Codes

- Hold the > Shift Key
- Click > F9
- Release both keys

Displays or hides all Fields in the document

- Hold the > Alt Key
- Click > F9
- Release both keys

Insert Field Braces

Section 9 – Extra

- Hold the > Ctrl Key
- Click > F9
- Release both keys

Converts codes to text value

- Hold the > Ctrl Key
- Hold the > Shift Key
- Click > F9
- Release all keys

Go to the next Field

- Click > F11
- Release

Go to the previous Field

- Hold the > Shift Key
- Click > F9
- Release both keys

Locks Fields

- Hold the > Ctrl Key
- Click > F11
- Release both keys

Unlocks fields

- Hold the > Ctrl Key
- Hold the > Shift Key

Section 9 – Extra

- Click > F11
- Release all keys

Building Blocks Organizer

Using the Building Blocks Organizer if an easy way to give your document structure although I have not used them much in government documents although once you have a cover or title page that you like you could save to the Building Blocks Organizer.

There are dozens of templates here that could make your documents look better but the only real way to see if there is something here that you would like to include in your document is to play around with this function.

The Building Blocks Organizer includes templates for

- Auto text
- Bibliographies
- Cover pages
- Equations
- Footers
- Headers

Section 9 – Extra

- Page Numbers
- Tables
- Tables of Contents
- Text Boxes
- Watermarks

www.ingramcontent.com/pod-product-compliance
Lightning Source LLC
Chambersburg PA
CBHW070807220526
45466CB00002B/576